"REDIGGING THE WEST"

FOR OLD TIME BOTTLES.

Revised Edition

by Lynn Blumenstein

Author of

"OLD TIME BOTTLES"
"BOTTLE RUSH U.S.A."
"WISHBOOK 1865"

Photographs of over 700
Ghost Town Bottles and
articles that can tell a
story.

PRICE $4.25
cc

Published by
OLD TIME BOTTLE PUBLISHING COMPANY
Salem, Oregon

ROBERT G. BLUMENSTEIN SR.
Photographer

© 1965 - 1966

COPYRIGHT 1965 BY
OLD TIME BOTTLE PUBLISHING COMPANY

Printed in the United States of America.

Library of Congress catalog card No. A776390
SBN No. 911068-03-1

TABLE OF CONTENTS

PREFACE

The real value of bottles of the past lies in the history of the bottle itself. There has been very little recorded concerning the common everyday life of those who ventured west in the 1800's. The bottles of these people become very important for gaining information. After a careful examination of an old refuse dump, the information obtained may reveal that the inhabitants were single, married with a family, or that they preferred one particular type of food over another, also, if they had been sick a great deal, and even the type of ailment. Through the many other articles found, more information and knowledge can be gained as to how these people lived. This same information could be obtained, if our refuse dumps were examined today. Many people have enjoyed reading about the hearty people of the 1800's, but in some ways this is not sufficient. Through bottle collecting, many individuals can enjoy possessing items that were used and cherished by those interesting people.

The author desires to share his own personal feelings through the following paragraph.

When tramping through the crumbling remains of a ghost town, I have visualized the people who came with high hopes when this land was new, just as God and time had fashioned it. Heard the creak of wagons, the ring of hammers, the thud of picks, the eager voices, all sound and movement; now silent except for my footsteps walking back in time and history. I have paused and heard the wind gently moving through the pines, and have heard the echoes of lost laughter.

Lynn Blumenstein

3

Bottles pictured from collections of:

Harold Hooper
Dick Weitzel
Dannie Simpson
Mr. & Mrs. Marion Marshall
Mr. & Mrs. Andy Shimko
Lynn & Barbara Blumenstein

SAGA OF THE WEST

With the shout of gold they came by the thousands, headlong into a way of life that would accept some and devour others. They became miners, farmers, and merchants while attempting to build a way of life that would have everlasting meaning.

Perhaps one of the most remembered was the miner. Here was a man with a zeal for adventure that almost surpassed himself. In his reckless search, he found that no matter how courageous he was, he had to constantly be aware of the fact, that he was just a mere particle in a surrounding that could crush him at a moment's notice. Knowing this he feared, as all men do, the unknown that laid ahead; however, he had been endowed with the stubborness of a mule, flavored with the fever for gold. In his lust for the riches of man, he would take on an entire mountain single-handed, and his faith would be constantly tested, as a mountain is a living, personal thing, he soon learned to love, hate and respect. He would burrow into his mountain, exposing a scar for all to view. With destruction always but a burning fuse away, many a timber would crumble, cracking out the word death; as the dust would settle, the mountain would grumble as if having difficulty digesting its toll; even so the miners were to believe that just under that thin mantle of earth was the Bonanza of Bonanzas. He would have to endure summers that would bake out the juices of sin, cleansing him for another round. Through the winters he would have to adjust to a coldness that would start within and work outward. As often as a comrade would lose the battle with his mountain, his fellow miners would make their trip to a freshly dug grave, on a now lonely mountain side, to stand with tears free of salt, made pure from the hurt within, staring at what now had become the ugly earth.

Now all are gone, but in their place are the remnants of dreams, and the ones who are present today in their surroundings can visualize their experiences.

The fragrance of the outdoors must not be taken into the nostrils lightly, rather, it must be drawn deeply into the lungs to a state of complete saturation, for then, and then only, will one understand the meaning of it all.

BOTTLE COLLECTING

Ghost town bottle collecting began with a minority group, who had a real eye for beauty. Their collecting ground ranged from the huge historical refuse dump of Virginia City, Nevada and the many forgotten mining towns of that state, onto the famous Mother Lode country of California, then further north to the states of Oregon, Washington, and Idaho, known for being rich in pioneer history. At first, the main collectable items were confined to Bitters bottles, Figural bottles, and all bottles that had turned the color amethyst through their long exposure to the warm violet rays of the sun.

As life became more complex in this world of today, many people began to look to our past for enjoyment. Many of us had already spent our free time enjoying the hobbies of rock hounding, hunting, fishing, and searching for Indian artifacts. People, who had previously paid little attention to the outdoors, headed into the wilderness by the thousands with the tide of the uranium rush. Soon camping, boating, and skin diving were as common as walking to the store. By the means of the Tote Gote, Honda, Trailster, etc., it became possible to further explore the back country. The average outdoorsman soon remembered where he had once seen an old bottle or two. The rock hound remembered the old mine dump where he had once collected rocks, but at that time he paid little attention to the refuse dump nearby. The hunter and fisherman recall that old cabin or homestead far out in the woods. The older generation are reminded of their childhood, old habits and where a certain article had been thrown out. Once again these people soon found a reason through bottle collecting to head back outdoors, only this time as a bottle detective.

Miner's stamp mill

Hand hewn cabin

Old deserted log cabin

Miner's church

10

LITTLE DIRGE FOR EVALENA

Sleep sleep, so fast in the soil of thy birth,

Rest, rest in peace, only God knows thy worth.

Rain, rain falling from above crushing the petals
   of each lovely flower;

Tears, tears falling their last for you in that
   bitter hour.

BOTTLE TERMS USED

Left to Right

1. Kickup   2. Turn mold, Opalescence
3. Wooden mold seam, Bubbles, Blob top
4. Embossed lettering,   Machine mold seam
5. Whittle mold   6. Graphite pontil
7. Open pontil

EMBOSSING	TYPE	SIZE	COLOR
Willmerding & Loewe Co. Kellogg's San Francisco, Cal.	Whiskey (inside screw threads)	12"	Amber
Kellogg's Nelson County, Extra Kentucky Bourbon Whiskey, W.L.C.O. Sole Agent	Whiskey (inside screw threads)	12"	Amber
The Rothenberg Co. Old Judge, Kentucky Whiskey, Trade Mark Reg. San Francisco, Cal.	Whiskey	11 1/2"	Amber
Trade Mark Old C.H. Moore Bourbon & Rye Jesse Moore & Co. Louisville, Ky. Moore-Hunt & Co. Sole Agents	Whiskey	12"	Amber

BOTTOM

EMBOSSING	TYPE	SIZE	COLOR
Full Measure Mail Order House F. Zimmerman & Co. Portland, Oregon	Whiskey	12 1/4"	Amber
Full Measure Mail Order House F. Zimmerman & Co. Portland, Oregon Net Contents 32 oz.	Whiskey	12"	Clear
High Grade Trade Mark Distilled for S. A. Arata & Co. Portland, Ore.	Whiskey (inside screw threads)	12 3/4"	Amethyst
Full Measure H. Varwig & Son Portland, Ore.	Whiskey (inside screw threads)	12 1/4"	Amber

TOP

EMBOSSING	TYPE	SIZE	COLOR
Crescent on Shoulder	Liquor	7 3/4"	Olive Green
Catto's Whiskey	Whiskey	9"	Olive Green
Crown Distilleries Company	Whiskey (inside screw threads)	11"	Amber
Paul Jones Whiskey Louisville, Ky.	Whiskey	9 1/2"	Amber

BOTTOM

W. J. Van Schuyver & Co. Portland	Whiskey	11 1/2"	Amber
The Duffy Malt Whiskey Company Rochester N.Y. U.S.A.	Whiskey	10"	Amber
The Rothenberg Co. Wholesale Liquor Dealers, San Francisco, Cal.	Whiskey	10 1/2"	Amber
The Rothenberg Co. Wholesale Liquor Dealers, San Francisco, Cal.	Whiskey	10 1/2"	Amber

EMBOSSING	TYPE	SIZE	COLOR
TOP			
Crescent on Shoulder	Brandy	10"	Amber
Plain	Brandy	9 1/4"	Amethyst
Wright & Taylor Distillers Louisville, Ky. Registered	Whiskey	9 3/4"	Amber
H. Guggenheimer & Bro. Distillers Cincinnati, O. U.S.A. Guaranteed Full Quart	Brandy	10"	Clear
BOTTOM			
Full Quart	Whiskey	10 1/4"	Amber
W. J. Van Schuyver & Co. Portland, Oregon Full Quart	Whiskey	10 1/4"	Amber
One Quart Full Measure	Whiskey	10 1/2"	Amber
Full Pint	Whiskey	8 3/4"	Amber

TOP

EMBOSSING	TYPE	SIZE	COLOR
Sunny Brook The Pure Food Whiskey Left Medallion Grand Prize St. Louis 1904 Right Medallion Gold Medal St. Louis 1904	Whiskey	10 3/4"	Clear
Plain	Decanter	11 3/4"	Amethyst
Old I. W. BB Harper	Whiskey Bar Bottle	10 3/4"	Crystal Clear
Plain	Whiskey Bar Bottle	11 1/4"	Crystal Clear

BOTTOM

EMBOSSING	TYPE	SIZE	COLOR
Hayner Whiskey Distillery Troy, Ohio	Whiskey	11 1/2"	Amethyst
Plain	Chicago Fancy Brandy	11 3/4"	Amethyst
Plain	Whiskey (inside screw threads)	10"	Amber
Plain	Chicago Fancy Brandy	10"	Ruby Red

EMBOSSING	TYPE	SIZE	COLOR
	TOP		
Dallemand & Co. Inc. Chicago	Brandy	11 1/2"	Amber
Shea Bocqueraz San Francisco, Cal.	Whiskey	11 3/4"	Amber
Plain	Brandy	9 1/4"	Amber
Plain	Brandy	8 1/2"	Amber
	BOTTOM		
Plain	Brandy	12"	Olive Green
Plain	Brandy	11 1/2"	Olive Green
Plain	Liquor	12"	Amber
Plain	Whiskey	11 1/2"	Amber

TOP

EMBOSSING	TYPE	SIZE	COLOR
Plain	(Madison Flask) Whiskey	8 1/2"	Amber
Flask	Whiskey	7 3/4"	Amber
Plain	(Eagle Flask) Whiskey	7 3/4"	Clear

BOTTOM

EMBOSSING	TYPE	SIZE	COLOR
The F. Chevalier Co. Whiskey Merchants San Francisco	Whiskey	7 3/4"	Amber
Simon Binswanger & Bro. W.L.CO. St. Joseph Mo.	Whiskey	6 3/4"	Clear
Devil's Islan Endurance Gin	Gin	7"	Clear
Flask	Liquor	5 3/4"	Golden Amber

EMBOSSING	TOP		
	TYPE	SIZE	COLOR
Plain	Whiskey Flask	6 1/2"	Amber
Plain	Whiskey Flask	6 1/4"	Amber
Plain	Madison Whiskey Flask	6 1/4"	Brown
Plain	Whiskey Flask	7 3/4"	Amber
	BOTTOM		
Plain	I. G. Ginger Liquor Flask	7 1/2"	Amethyst
Plain	I.G. Ginger	7 1/4"	Clear
Warranted Flask	Liquor	6 1/2"	Clear
Warranted	Liquor	8"	Amethyst

EMBOSSING	TOP		
	TYPE	SIZE	COLOR
Plain	Union Oval Liquor Flask	8"	Amber
Plain	Union Oval Liquor Flask	6 1/4"	Amber
Plain	Liquor Flask	6 1/4"	Amber
Plain	Union Oval Liquor Flask	6"	Amber

	BOTTOM		
J.H. Cutter Old Bourbon A.P. Hotaling & Co. Portland, O	Shoo-Fly Whiskey Flask	7 3/4"	Amber
Plain	Shoo-Fly Whiskey Flask	6"	Amber
The North Pole Anderson Bros. 722 Maynard Ave. Seattle, Wash. Full 1/2 Pint	Whiskey Flask	7"	Clear
Plain	Cummings Picnic Flask	6"	Green Tint

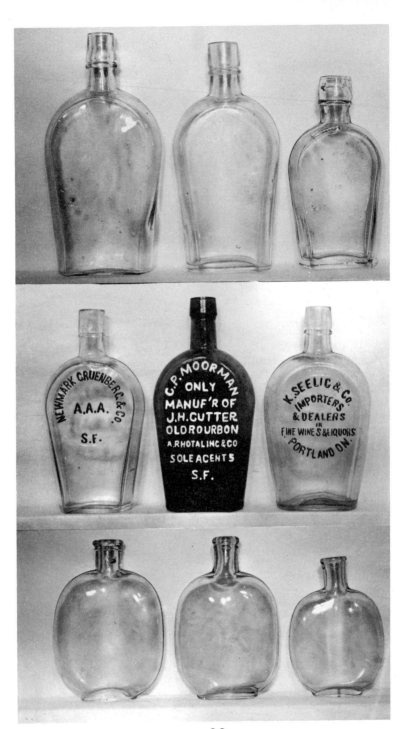

TOP

EMBOSSING	TYPE	SIZE	COLOR
Plain	Shoo-Fly Whiskey Flask	7 5/8"	Clear
Plain	Shoo-Fly Whiskey Flask	7 1/8"	Clear
Plain	Shoo-Fly Whiskey Flask	6"	Clear

MIDDLE

EMBOSSING	TYPE	SIZE	COLOR
Newmark Gruenberg & Co. A.A.A. S.F.	Shoo-Fly Whiskey Flask	7 1/4"	Clear
C. P. Moorman Only Manuf'r of J.H. Cutter Old Bourbon A.P. Hotaling & Co. Sole Agents S.F.	Shoo-Fly Whiskey Flask	7 1/2"	Gold
K. Seelig & Co. Importers & Dealers Fine Wine & Liquors Portland, ON.	Shoo-Fly Whiskey Flask	7 1/2"	Clear

BOTTOM

EMBOSSING	TYPE	SIZE	COLOR
Plain	Picnic Whiskey Flask	6 3/8"	Amethyst
Plain	Picnic Whiskey Flask	5 1/2"	Amethyst
Plain	Picnic Whiskey Flask	4 1/2"	Amethyst

TOP

EMBOSSING	TYPE	SIZE	COLOR
L. Rose & Co. LTD	Limewater	11 1/8"	Pale Green
L. Rose & Co. LTD	Limewater	14"	Pale Green
Dr. C. Bouvier's Buchu Gin	Gin	11 3/4"	Clear
Plain	Gin	10"	Clear

BOTTOM

EMBOSSING	TYPE	SIZE	COLOR
Garrett & Co. Established 1835 American Wines Norfolk, Va. St. Louis Mo. Registered Trade Mark Refilling Prohibited	Wine	13"	Clear
Property of Mc Connan Smith Limited-Vancouver, B.C.	Liquor	11 1/4"	Amethyst
Plain	(Sandwich Glass)	11 1/8"	Jade Green
Amidons Union Ginger Brandy Registered	Brandy	11 3/4"	Clear

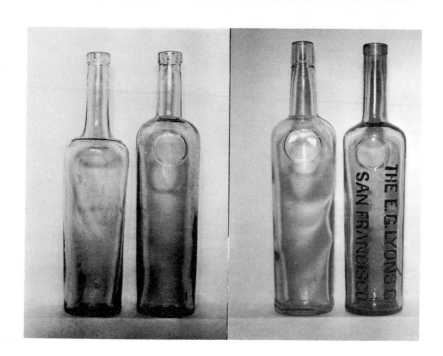

TOP

EMBOSSING	TYPE	SIZE	COLOR
Cresent	Brandy	11 1/2"	Green
Cresent	Brandy	11 5/8"	Amethyst
Cresent	Brandy	12"	Amethyst
Cresent The E.G.Lyons Co. San Francisco	Brandy	12"	Amethyst

BOTTOM

EMBOSSING	TYPE	SIZE	COLOR
Plain	Liquor	11 3/4"	Green
Plain	Brandy	11"	Clear
Gordon's Dry Gin London England	Gin	8 1/2"	Aqua
Plain	Taper Gin	6 1/2"	Avacado Green

TOP

EMBOSSING	TYPE	SIZE	COLOR
As shown	Hocks Wine	14"	Amber
Plain	Hocks Wine	14"	Dark Amber
4/5 Quart	Hocks Wine	14"	Amber

BOTTOM

Plain	Wine	11 1/4"	Green
Plain	Wine	9 3/4"	Green
Plain	Wine	8"	Jade

	TOP		
EMBOSSING	TYPE	SIZE	COLOR
Plain	Wine	11 3/4"	Green
Plain	Wine	9 1/2"	Olive Green
Plain	Wine	8"	Green
	BOTTOM		
Plain	Champagne	12"	Green
Plain	Champagne	10"	Green Opalescent
Plain	Champagne	9"	Green Opalescent

39

	TOP		
EMBOSSING	TYPE	SIZE	COLOR
Reno Brewing Co. Reno Nev.	Beer	11"	Brown
American Brewing & C.I. Co. Baker City, Ore.	Beer	11 1/4"	Brown
Enterprise Brewing Co. S. F. Cal.	Beer	12 1/2"	Brown
K.C.B.C.	Beer	12"	Brown
	BOTTOM		
Buffalo Brewing Co. Sacramento, Cal.	Beer	11 3/4"	Brown
Lion Brewery LTD. Registered Trade Mark Auckland Lion Ale & Stout This Bottle is the Property of the Lion Brewery LTD.	Ale	11 3/4"	Brown
Plain	Liquor	11 3/4"	Black Glass (Olive Green)
Plain	Liquor	8"	Black Glass (Olive Green)

TOP

EMBOSSING	TYPE	SIZE	COLOR
Plain	Brandy	9 3/4"	Olive Green
Plain	Wine	9"	Jade
Plain	Beverage	9 3/4"	Green
Plain	Wine	9 1/2"	Olive Green

BOTTOM

Aberdeen BR'W'G. Co. Aberdeen, Wash.	Beer	9 1/4"	Brown
Star Brewery Vancouver, Wash.	Beer	11 3/4"	Brown
Claussen BREW'G ASS'N Seattle, Wash.	Beer	9 1/2"	Brown
The Victor Brewing Co. Jeannette, Pa.	Beer	9 3/4"	Brown

EMBOSSING	TYPE	SIZE	COLOR
	TOP		
Plain	Pabst Beer	9 1/4"	Brown
Chinese lettering	Unknown	9"	Dark Brown
Blatz, Milwaukee	Beer	9 1/4"	Olive Drab
Plain	Beer	8 3/4"	Amber
	BOTTOM		
Pine & Co. Seattle, Washington Home Brewed Ginger Beer	Ginger Beer	7"	Pottery
Cross & Co. LTD. Ginger Beer Vancouver, B.C.	Ginger Beer	7 1/4"	Pottery
Ginger Victoria Beer Brewed By Old English Beverage Co. LTD. Victoria B.C. Minimum Contents 10 Fluid Ounces	Ginger Beer	7 5/8"	Pottery
C.W. Abbott & Co. Baltimore	Bitters	8 1/4"	Brown

EMBOSSING	TOP		
	TYPE	SIZE	COLOR
Plain	Beer	11 1/4"	Blue
Plain	Beer	11 3/4"	Blue
Plain	Beer	11 1/4"	Clear
Plain	Beer	11 1/2"	Amber
	BOTTOM		
Plain	Whiskey	11"	Amethyst
Plain	Liquor	12"	Amber
Plain	Liquor	12 1/4"	Green Opalescent
Plain	Beer	11 1/4"	Light Green

47

EMBOSSING	TYPE	SIZE	COLOR
S T Drake 1860 Plantation X Bitters Patented 1862	Bitters	10"	Amber
Dr. C. W. Robacks Stomach Bitters Cincinnati, O.	Bitters	9 3/4"	Dark Brown
Electric Brand Bitters H.E. Bucklen & Co. Chicago, ILL.	Bitters	10"	Amber
Doyles Hop Bitters 1872	Bitters	11 1/4"	Amber

BOTTOM

Dr. Henley's Wild Grape Root IXL Bitters	Bitters	12 1/4"	Aqua
Peruvian Bitters Shield with WKC	Bitters	9"	Dark Brown
As shown (Carp)	Cod Liver Oil	9 3/4"	Amber
Orizaba Bitters J. Maristany JR.	Bitters	8 1/2"	Brown

49

TOP

EMBOSSING	TYPE	SIZE	COLOR
Lash's Bitters Co. San Francisco, Calif.	Bitters	11 1/2"	Amber
Lash's Bitters Co. N.Y. Chicago S.F.	Bitters	11 1/2"	Amber
Dr. J. Hostetter's Stomach Bitters	Bitters	9"	Amber
Lash's Kidney & Liver Bitters, The best Cathartic and Blood Purifier	Bitters	8 3/4"	Amber

BOTTOM

EMBOSSING	TYPE	SIZE	COLOR
J.A. Gilka Berlin Schutzon STR. NO. 9	Liquor	9 3/4"	Brown
Cresent	Liquor (Benedicktine)	10 1/4"	Olive Green
Munyon's Paw Paw	Tonic	10"	Brown
Homers California Ginger Brandy	Brandy	11 1/4"	Amber

EMBOSSING	TOP TYPE	SIZE	COLOR
Gold Lion Iron Tonic	Tonic	8 3/4"	Amber
Celro-Kola	Tonic	8 3/4"	Amber
Warner's Safe Kidney & Liver Cure Rochester, N.Y.	Cure	9 3/4"	Amber
Paines Celery Compound	Compound	9 1/2"	Amber

BOTTOM

Foley's Sarsaparilla Mfd. by Foley & Co. Chicago	Sarsaparilla	9 1/4"	Amber
Moore's Revealed Remedy	Remedy	9"	Amber
Frederick Stearns & Co. Detroit Mich.	Tonic	10 1/4"	Amber
Prima Tonic Registered Property of Independent BR'G Asso. Chicago, ILL.	Tonic	7 1/2"	Amber

EMBOSSING	TOP TYPE	SIZE	COLOR
EJB (on bottom)	Tonic or Bitters	9"	Amber
Plain	Tonic or Bitters	8 3/4"	Amber
Plain	Bitters or Brandy	11 1/2"	Amber
Dr. S.B.H. & Co. PR. (on bottom)	Tonic	9 1/4"	Aqua
	BOTTOM		
Plain	Gin	11"	Amethyst
Plain	Whiskey	12"	Amber
Dr. Greene's Sarsaparilla	Sarsaparilla	9 "	Aqua
Hood's Compound Extract Sarsaparilla	Sarsaparilla	8 3/4"	Aqua

	TOP		
EMBOSSED	TYPE	SIZE	COLOR
Buffalo Luthia Water Natures Nateria Medica Trade Mark	Mineral Water	11 1/2"	Aqua
Abilene Natural Cathartic Water (on bottom)	Mineral Water	11 1/2"	Brown
Saxlehners Hunyaoi Janos Bitterquelle (on bottom)	Mineral Water	10 1/2"	Avacado Green
	BOTTOM		
Shasta Water Co.	Mineral Water	10 1/2"	Brown
Pluto Water America's Physic	Mineral Water	10 1/4"	Green
Veronica	Mineral Water	9 1/2"	Brown

TOP

EM BOSSING	TYPE	SIZE	COLOR
Sol Duc Hot Springs Co. Sol Duc Natural Spring Water Sol Duc, Wash.	Mineral Water	14"	Green
Oregon Importing Co. We Neither Rectify Nor Compound Portland, Ore.	Mineral Water	14"	Green

BOTTOM

Plain	Mineral Water	14"	Brown
Plain	Poland Water	13 3/4"	Green

TOP

EMBOSSING	TYPE	SIZE	COLOR
Plain Pottery	Ale	8 1/2"	Brown & White
Plain Pottery	Ale	8 3/4"	White
Plain	Wine	12 1/2"	Green
Plain	Ale	11 1/2"	White

BOTTOM

Plain Porcelain	Sake	11 1/2"	White
Plain Pottery	Wine	9 1/4"	Brick Red
Plain Pottery	Mineral Water	12"	Rust
Plain Pottery	Mineral Water	11 3/4"	Rust

TOP

EMBOSSING	TYPE	SIZE	COLOR
Plain	Beverage	9"	Green
Plain	Beverage	9 5/8"	Clear
Plain	Beverage	9 1/4"	Green
Plain	Beverage	9"	Aqua

BOTTOM

EMBOSSING	TYPE	SIZE	COLOR
Highrock Congress Springs C & W Saratoga, N.Y.	Mineral Water	8"	Black Glass (Olive Green)
Champion Spouting Spring Saratoga Mineral Spring Co. Limited, Saratoga N.Y.	Mineral Water	7 1/2"	Aqua
Nichols Flushing L.I. Union Glass Works Philad.	Soda	7 1/4"	Dark Jade
Trade Mark Registered Johnson Liverpool	Mineral Water	9"	Olive Green
Crown	Mineral Water	8 1/2"	Black Glass (Olive Green)

EMBOSSING	TYPE	SIZE	COLOR
Plain	Pop	8 1/2"	Aqua
See that each cork is branded Cantrell & Cochrane Dublin & Belfast	Pop	9 1/2"	Aqua
Canada Dry Ginger Ale Incorporated (on bottom)	Ginger Ale	9 3/4"	Carnival Glass
Florida Water Murray & Lanman Druggists New York	Medical	9"	Aqua

BOTTOM

Barry Brothers 323 E. 38th St. New York	Ginger Ale	11 1/4"	Aqua
Registered Connecticut Breweries Co. Bridgeport, Conn. This bottle not to be sold	Ginger Ale	9"	Aqua
Beadleston & Woerz Excelsior Empire Brewery New York This bottle not to be sold	Beer	9"	Aqua
Phillips Soda Springs Natural Mineral Water Phillips Napa Co. Soda	Mineral Water	8"	Aqua

EMBOSSING	TYPE	SIZE	COLOR
TOP			
Pacific Soda Works Portland, Oregon	Soda	8 3/4"	Aqua
Western Trade Mark Reg. Soda Works P.O.	Soda	7"	Blue
The Northrop & Sturgis Company Portland, Oregon	Soda	6 1/2"	Blue
Plain	Soda	6 5/8"	Aqua
BOTTOM			
Seattle Soda Works	Soda	7"	Aqua
C.H. Martin & Co. Soda Works Avon, Wash.	Soda	7"	Blue
Pioneer Trade Mark Soda Works P.O.	Soda	6 1/4"	Aqua
Rainier Soda & Bottling Works Seattle, Wash.	Soda	7"	Aqua

EMBOSSING	TOP TYPE	SIZE	COLOR
Woodburn Bottling Works Woodburn, Oregon	Soda	8 1/2"	Aqua
Star Bottling Works Salem, Oregon	Soda	8 1/4"	Aqua
Standard Soda Works McMinnville, Ore.	Soda	8 1/4"	Aqua
Plain	Soda	8 1/2"	Blue
BOTTOM			
Coca Cola Co. Seattle, Wash.	Beverage	8 1/4"	Aqua
Fox Trade Mark J.C. Fox & Co. Seattle, Wash.	Soda	7 3/4"	Aqua
Alvan Valey Bottling Works Everett, Wash.	Soda	8 1/4"	Aqua
Zarembo Mineral Springs Co. Seattle, Wash.	Mineral Water	7 1/4"	Blue

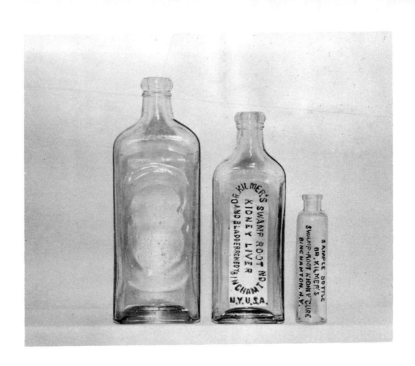

TOP

EMBOSSING	TYPE	SIZE	COLOR
Plain	Remedy	8 1/4"	Blue
Dr. Kilmers Swamp Root Kidney Liver and Bladder Remedy Binghamton N.Y. U.S.A.	Remedy	7"	Aqua
Sample Bottle Dr. Kilmers Swamp Root Kidney Cure Binghamton N.Y.	Cure	4 1/2"	Aqua

BOTTOM

EMBOSSING	TYPE	SIZE	COLOR
The Great Dr. Kilmer's Swamp Root Kidney Liver & Bladder Cure, Specific	Cure	8 1/4"	Blue
The Great Dr. Kilmer's Swamp Root Kidney Liver & Bladder Remedy	Remedy	8 1/4"	Aqua
Dr. Kilmers Swamp Root Kidney Liver & Bladder Remedy	Remedy	8 1/4"	Aqua

TOP

EMBOSSING	TYPE	SIZE	COLOR
Scotts Emulsion	Consumption medicine	7 1/2"	Aqua
J.E. Gombault's Caustic Balsam	Horse & Cattle Medicine	6 1/4"	Aqua
Parker's Hair Balsam New York	Hair Grooming	7 1/2"	Brown
Hay's Hair Health	Hair Grooming	7 1/2"	Brown

BOTTOM

Dr. S. Pitcher's Castoria	Laxative	5 3/4"	Aqua
Chas. H. Fletcher's Castoria	Laxative	5 7/8"	Blue
California Fig Syrup Co.	Laxative	7"	Clear
California Fig Syrup Co. San Francisco Cal.	Laxative	7"	Clear
California Fig Syrup Co. Califig Sterling Products (Inc) Successor	Laxative	7"	Clear

EMBOSSING	TYPE	SIZE	COLOR
Dr. King's New Discovery For Consumption	Medical	6 3/4"	Aqua
Dr. King's New Discovery Coughs and Colds	Medical	6 3/4"	Aqua
Dr. Thacher's Liver and Blood Syrup Chattanooga, Tenn.	Medical	8"	Aqua
Dr. D. Jayne's Tonic Vermifuge 242 Chest. St. Phila.	Medical	5 1/2"	Aqua
Dr. D. Jayne's Tonic Vermifuge 242 Chest. St. Phila.	Medical	5 1/2"	Blue

BOTTOM

Chamberlain's Colic And Diarrhea Remedy	Medical	4 3/8"	Aqua
Chamberlain's Colic Cholera Diarrehea Remedy	Medical	4 1/2"	Aqua
De Witts Colic & Cholera Cure	Medical	4 7/8"	Blue
Pond's Extract 1846	Medical	5 3/8"	Aqua
Ayers	Medical	6 1/4"	Aqua

EMBOSSING	TYPE	SIZE	COLOR
N.L. Clark & Co. Peruvian Syrup	Medical	8 1/2"	Aqua
Henleys Royal Balsom	Medical	6 3/4"	Amethyst
Gargling Oil Lockport N Y	Medical	7"	Green
Halls Balsam For the Lungs A.L. Scovill Co. Cin'ti & N. Y.	Medical	7 1/2"	Blue
Dr. J. H. McLeans Volcanic Liniment Oil	Medical	9"	Aqua

BOTTOM

Smith Drug Co. Second & James Seattle, Wash.	Medical	5 1/2"	Clear
Piso's Cure For Consumption Hazeltine & Co.	Medical	5 1/4"	Aqua
Piso's Cure For Consumption Hazeltine & Co.	Medical	5 1/4"	Green
Optimus Stewart & Holmes Drug Co. Seattle, Wash.	Medical	6 1/2"	Aqua
Dr. A. Bochee's German Syrup	Consumption Cure	6 3/4"	Aqua

EMBOSSING	TYPE	SIZE	COLOR
	TOP		
The Maltine MF'G Co. Chemists New York	Medical	7 1/2"	Brown
Reed and Carnrick Pharmacists New York	Medical	7 1/2"	Golden Amber
Schlotterbeck & Foss Co. One Fluid Pint Portland, Maine	Medical	7 1/2"	Brown
Hydrozone Prepared only By Chas Marchand New York U.S.A.	Medical	8 1/2"	Brown
	BOTTOM		
Wyeth 217 (on bottom)	Medical	9 1/4"	Dark Brown
Plain	Medical	7 1/2"	Dark Brown
Purola Trade Mark Regd.	Toilet Preparation	8 1/4"	Brown
Plain	Medical	8"	Brown

EMBOSSING	TYPE	SIZE	COLOR
	TOP		
WM. R. Warner & Co. New York St. Louis	Medical	7 1/8"	Amber
Dr. D. Jayne's Alterative 242 Chest. St. Phila.	Medical	6 5/8"	Aqua
Prescribed By R.V. Pierce M.D. Buffalo N.Y.	Medical	7"	Aqua
India Cholagogue Osgood's Norwich, Conn. U.S.A.	Medical (for liver & Bile)	5 1/4"	Aqua
	BOTTOM		
Woodard Clark & Co. Chemists Portland, Or.	Medical	7 1/8"	Amethyst
Woodard Clark & Co. Chemists Portland, Or.	Medical	5 3/4"	Amethyst
Woodard Clark & Co. Chemists Portland, Or.	Medical	5"	Amethyst
O D Chem Co. New York	Medical	6 3/8"	Brown
Thymus	Medical	4"	Brown

EMBOSSING	TYPE	SIZE	COLOR
TOP			
Plain	Rexall Drug	8 1/2"	Dark Brown
Plain	Rexall Drug	6 1/8"	Dark Brown
Plain	Rexall Drug	4 3/4"	Dark Brown
Plain	Rexall Drug	3 3/8"	Dark Brown
BOTTOM			
Ablmyersam Rock Rose New Haven	Medical	9 1/8"	Dark Jade Green
Dr. Kaufmann's Sulphur Bitters	Bitters	8 1/4"	Aqua
Burdock Blood Bitters	Bitters	7 1/2"	Aqua
Ayers Sarsaparilla Lowell Mass. U.S.A. Compound Ext.	Sarsaparilla	8 1/2"	Aqua

TOP

EMBOSSING	TYPE	SIZE	COLOR
W.H. Hooker & Co. Proprietors New York, U.S.A. Ackers English Remedy For the Throat & Lungs	Medical	4 3/4"	Cobalt
Laxol A J White New York Design Patented April 10 1894	Medical	7"	Cobalt
Wm. R. Warner & Co. Philadelphia.	Medical	5 3/4"	Cobalt
John Wyeth & Bro. Next Dose (Numbers 1 to 12)	Medical	6 3/4"	Cobalt
Wisdoms Robertine	Lotion	5"	Cobalt

BOTTOM

EMBOSSING	TYPE	SIZE	COLOR
As Shown	Poison	7"	Cobalt
As Shown	Poison	5 1/2"	Cobalt
As Shown	Poison	4 1/2"	Cobalt
Poison	Poison	3 1/4"	Cobalt
Poison	Poison	2 3/4"	Amber
Poison (3-cornered)	Poison	2 1/2"	Cobalt

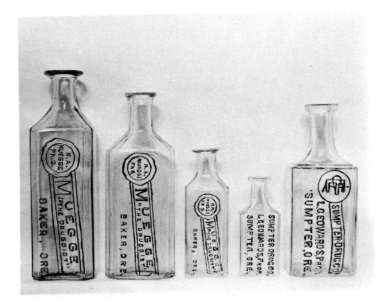

TOP

EMBOSSING	TYPE	SIZE	COLOR
Osseward Pharmacy Cobb Bldg. Seattle	Medical	7"	Clear
Osseward Pharmacy Cobb Bldg. Seattle	Medical	6 1/4"	Clear
K - B Clemens Sells Drugs & Books	Medical	6"	Clear
Buckeye Extract Co. Olympia, Wash.	Extract	5 5/8"	Clear
Buckeye Extract Co. Olympia, Wash.	Extract	4 5/8"	Clear

BOTTOM

EMBOSSING	TYPE	SIZE	COLOR
N.A. Muegge Ph. G. Muegge The Druggist Baker, Ore.	Medical	6 7/8"	Amethyst
N.A. Muegge Ph. G. Muegge The Druggist Baker, Ore.	Medical	6 1/8"	Clear
N.A. Muegge Ph. G. Muegge The Druggist Baker, Ore.	Medical	4 1/4"	Clear
Sumpter Drug Co. L.C. Edwards. Prop. Sumpter, Ore.	Medical	3 3/8"	Clear
Sumpter Drug Co. L.C. Edwards, Prop. Sumpter, Ore.	Medical	5 3/8"	Clear

TOP

EMBOSSING	TYPE	SIZE	COLOR
Kennedy's Rheumatic Liniment Dr. Kennedys Roxbury, Mass.	Liniment	6 1/2"	Aqua
Hoff's German Liniment Goodrich & Jennings Anoka, Minn.	Liniment	7"	Amethyst
Hoff's Liniment Goodrich Drug Co. Anoka, Minn.	Liniment	5 1/2"	Amethyst
Kendall's Spavin Cure For Human Flesh	Medical	5 1/2"	Aqua
St. Jakobs Oel St. Jacobs Oil LTD. Baltimore, MD. U.S.A.	Medical	6 1/4"	Clear

BOTTOM

EMBOSSING	TYPE	SIZE	COLOR
Special Battery Oil Thomas A. Edison Incorporated Primary Battery Division Bloomfield, N.J. U.S.A.	Oil	4 3/4"	Clear
Hamlin's Wizard Oil	Oil	6 1/4"	Aqua
Sylmar Brand Los Angeles Olive Growers Assn. Los Angeles, Cal.	Olive Oil	10"	Amethyst
Three In One Oil Three In One	Oil	5 1/4"	Blue
Three In One Oil Three In One	Oil	3 3/4"	Aqua

EMBOSSING	TOP TYPE	SIZE	COLOR
Dr. Peter's Kuriko Prepared By Dr. Peter Fahrney & Sons Co. Chicago, ILL. U.S.A.	Medical	9"	Clear
Plain	Medical	8 3/4"	Amber
Boericket & Runyon Company	Medical	7 3/4"	Clear
Armour Laboratories Chicago	Medical	7 3/4"	Amber

	BOTTOM		
Lydia E. Pinkham's Vegetable Compound	Compound	8 3/8"	Aqua
Fellows Syrup of Hypophosphites	Medical	7 3/4"	Blue
Lorrimer Medical Institute Inc. Baltimore, MD.	Medical	6 1/4"	Brown
6 OZ. Mary T. Goldman St. Paul, Minn.	Medical	5 1/2"	Amber

EMBOSSING	TYPE	SIZE	COLOR
The Celebrated H.H.H. Horse Liniment DDT 1868	Liniment	7"	Aqua
Rheumatic Liniment	Liniment	6 3/4"	Aqua
Dr. A. Boschees German Syrup	Medical	6 3/4"	Aqua
Reed & Carnrick, N.Y. Siphon Kumysgen Bottle For Preparing Kumyss From Kumysgen Use 7 Tablets	Kumysgen	6 3/4"	Green
Dickey Chemist Pioneer 1850 S.F.	Medical	5 3/4"	Cobalt

BOTTOM

Gargling Oil Lockport, N.Y.	Medical	5 5/8"	Green
The Piso Company Trade Mark Pisos Hazeltine & Co.	Medical	5 1/2"	Brown
The Piso Company Trade Mark Pisos Hazeltine & Co.	Medical	5 1/4"	Emerald Green
Buckingham Whisker Dye	Dye	4 3/4"	Brown
C. Damschinsky Liquid Hair Dye New York	Dye	3 1/2"	Aqua

TOP

EMBOSSING	TYPE	SIZE	COLOR
Citrate of Magnesia	Laxative	8"	Amethyst
Citrate of Magnesia	Laxative	8"	Clear
Citrate of Magnesia	Laxative	7 3/4"	Clear
Citrate of Magnesia	Laxative	8 1/4"	Amethyst

BOTTOM

Purola	Toilet Preparation	7 1/2"	Amethyst
Purola	Toilet Preparation	6 3/4"	Amethyst
Purola	Toilet Preparation	5 3/4"	Amethyst
Purola	Toilet Preparation	4 5/8"	Amethyst

TOP

EMBOSSING	TYPE	SIZE	COLOR
Dr. W.B. Caldwell's Syrup Pepsin	Medical	9"	Green
Dr. W.B. Caldwell's Monticello, Illinois	Medical	9"	Green
Caldwell's Syrup Pepsin MF'd By Pepsin Syrup Company Monticello, Illinois.	Medical	7 1/8"	Aqua
Dr. W. B. Caldwell's Monticello, Illinois	Medical	7"	Green

BOTTOM

McElrees Wine of Cardui Chattanooga Medical Co.	Medical	8 1/2"	Aqua
R.V. Pierce, M.D. Buffalo, N.Y.	Medical	9"	Aqua
Dr. Pierce's Golden Medical Discovery R.V. Pierce, M.D. Buffalo, N.F.	Medical	8 1/4"	Aqua
S.B. Dr. Vanderpool's Headache and Liver Cure	Medical	8"	Aqua

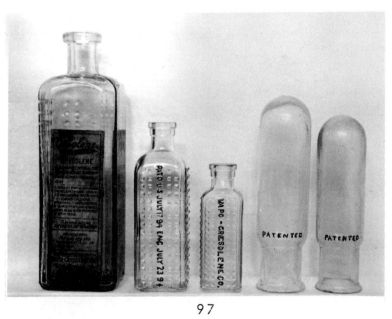

EMBOSSING	TYPE	SIZE	COLOR
Chamberlain's Pain Balm	Medical	5 1/4"	Aqua
Rennes Magic Oil Pain Killing	Medical	5 7/8"	Blue
Chamberlain's Pain Balm	Medical	7 1/8"	Blue
Davis Vegetable Pain killer	Medical	6 5/8"	Aqua
Davis Vegetable Pain killer	Medical	6 1/8"	Blue

BOTTOM

Vapo-Cresolene Co. Patd. U.S. July 17,94 Eng. July 23, 94	Vaporizer	8"	Clear
Vapo-Cresolene Co. Patd. U.S. July 17,94 Eng. July 23,94	Vaporizer	5 1/4"	Clear
Vapo-Cresolene Co. Patd. U.S. July 17,94 Eng. July 23,94	Vaporizer	4"	Clear
Patented	Olive	6"	Clear
Patented	Olive	5 1/2"	Clear

TOP

EMBOSSING	TYPE	SIZE	COLOR
Plain (Over 100 Year Old)	Snuff	4 1/2"	Amber
Glycerole	Unknown	5"	Blue
Pik-Ron Trade Mark Wolff & Randolph Philadelphia	Unknown	5 1/8"	Blue
French Gloss Whittemore Boston	Shoe Polish	4 5/8"	Blue
Oriental Cream Couraud's New York	Lotion	5"	Amethyst

BOTTOM

EMBOSSING	TYPE	SIZE	COLOR
Absorbine $2.00 Per Bottle M'F'G. By W.F. Young P.O.E. Springfield, Mass. U.S.A.	Liniment	7 1/2"	Brown
Plain	Medical	7 1/2"	Brown
We Neither Rectify Nor Compound Oregon Importing Co. Portland, Ore.	Unknown	9 3/8"	Amber
Plain	Medical	7 1/4"	Brown

EMBOSSING	TYPE	SIZE	COLOR
U.S. Public Health Service 125 cc	Medical	5 1/4	Clear
Skabcura Dip Co. Chicago U.S.A.	Sheep Dip	4 1/4"	Aqua
Kutnows Powder	Unknown	4 3/4"	Blue
Plain	Snuff	4"	Amber
Doct Marshall's Catarrh Snuff	Snuff	3 1/4"	Aqua

BOTTOM

EMBOSSING	TYPE	SIZE	COLOR
Owl Trade Mark Pharmaceuticals Standard	Medical	8"	Amethyst
The Owl Drug Co.	Medical	6"	Clear
The Owl Drug Co.	Medical	6"	Clear
The Owl Drug Co.	Medical	5"	Milk Glass

TOP

EMBOSSING	TYPE	SIZE	COLOR
Chas. Dennehy & Co. Chicago	Unknown	5 1/4"	Amber
Wakelee's Camelline	Skin Lotion	4 3/4"	Brown
Medical Department U.S.N.	Medical	5"	Brown
Dr. Bosankos Cough and Lungs Syrup Piqua, Ohio U.S.A. The Dr. Bosanko Medicine Co.	Medical	6"	Blue
Carbona Marshall Chemical Co. Carbona	Medical	6 1/4"	Blue

BOTTOM

Plain	Sample Whiskey	3"	Amber
Dallemand & Co. Cream Rye	Sample Whiskey	2 3/4"	Amber
Pa-Pay-ans Bell Bell Co. Inc. New York U.S.A.	Naseau Pills	2 3/4"	Amber
Hannis Distilling Co Re-Use Prohibited	Liquor	4 7/8"	Amber

EMBOSSING	TYPE	SIZE	COLOR

TOP

EMBOSSING	TYPE	SIZE	COLOR
Plain	Perfume	3 1/2"	Amethyst
Plain (Pouring Lip)	Medical	3 1/8"	Amber
Mrs. Potters Hygienic Supply Co. Cincinnati, Ohio No.1	Medical	3 7/8"	Amber
Plain	Perfume	2 1/2"	Clear
Hood's Pills Dose 1 to 4 Cure Liver Ills G.I. Hood & Co. Lowell, Mass.	Medical	1 7/8"	Clear
Dr. Kings New Discovery Rhumatic Liniment Roxbury, Mass.	Liniment	4 1/8"	Blue
Plain	Medical	4 3/8"	Aqua
Dr. Le Gear's Liniment St. Louis, Mo.	Liniment	4 1/8"	Amber

MIDDLE

EMBOSSING	TYPE	SIZE	COLOR
Sample Bottle Dr. Kilmers Swamp Root	Medical	3"	Aqua
Foley & Co.	Medical	3 1/2"	Clear
Plain	Perfume	3"	Clear
Glyco-Thymoline	Medical	2 1/4"	Clear
First	Medical	2"	Clear
Plain	Unknown	2"	Aqua
Plain	Smelling Salts	1 3/4"	Clear

BOTTOM

EMBOSSING	TYPE	SIZE	COLOR
Preston Of New Hampshire	Smelling Salts	2 3/4"	Cobalt
Atrask	Ointment	2 1/2"	Aqua
Plain	Pills	5 1/4"	Aqua
Dr. Thompson's Eye Water New London, Conn.	Eye Water	3 3/4"	Aqua
Gerroeders Waaning Tilly	Pills	3 3/8"	Aqua
Dr. Sraca's Cuban Vermifuge	Vermifuge	3 3/4"	Aqua
Plain	Opium	2 1/4"	Aqua
Plain	Unknown	2"	Amethyst
Plain	Unknown	1 1/4"	Cobalt

EMBOSSING	TYPE	SIZE	COLOR
Palmers	Perfume	5 1/4"	Emerald Green
Dabrooks' Detroit Perfumers	Perfume	6"	Amethyst
Frostilla	Cosmetic	4 3/8"	Clear
Hoyt's German Cologne L.W. Hoyt & Co. Lowell, Mass	Cologne	3 1/2"	Amethyst
Ed Pinaud Paris	Perfume	2 3/8"	Clear

MIDDLE

EMBOSSING	TYPE	SIZE	COLOR
Lubin Parfumeur Paris	Perfume	3"	Clear
Plain	Perfume	3 1/2"	Clear
Plain	Perfume	3 1/2	Clear
Plain	Perfume	2"	Clear
Plain	Perfume	3 1/2"	Clear
Eau Dentifrice Du Docteur Jeaa Paris	Unknown	3"	Clear

BOTTOM

EMBOSSING	TYPE	SIZE	COLOR
Depose Guerlain Paris	Perfume	3 1/4"	Clear
Plain	Perfume	3 1/2"	Clear
Plain	Perfume	3 1/4"	Clear
Plain	Perfume	2 1/4"	Clear
Lazell	Perfume	2 1/2"	Clear
Plain	Perfume	3"	Clear

EMBOSSING	TYPE	SIZE	COLOR
Pompeian Cream Made By Pompeian MFG. Cleveland, Ohio	Cream	2 7/8"	Amethyst
Pompeian Massage Cream	Cream	2 3/4"	Clear
J.R. Watkins Medical Company Winona, Minn. U.S.A.	Unknown	3 3/8"	Amethyst
Bixby Pattented MCH. 6,83	Shoe Polish	3 3/8"	Brown
B & Co.	Paste	3"	Amethyst

MIDDLE

Buchan's Hungarian Balsam of Life London	Kidney Cure	5 3/4"	Green
Turner's Ess Of Jamaica Ginger, New York	Ginger	5 3/4"	Clear
E.G. Lyons & Co. Ess. Jamica Ginger S.F.	Ginger	6"	Clear
W.T. Wenzell San Francisco	Unknown	5 1/2"	Clear
Atwoods Jaundice Bitters Formerly Made By Moses Atwood	Bitters	6"	Clear

BOTTOM

Milk Weed Cream	Cream	2 1/2"	Milk Glass
Plain	Cream	3"	Milk Glass
Plain	Menthol	2 3/8"	Milk Glass
Plain	Ads Peroxide	2 1/8"	Milk Glass
Plain	Cream	2 3/4"	Milk Glass

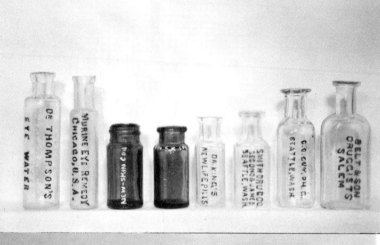

EMBOSSING	TYPE	SIZE	COLOR
	TOP		
Dr. Thompsons Eye Water	Eye Water	3 3/4"	Aqua
Murine Eye Remedy Chicago U.S.A.	Eye Water	3 3/4"	Aqua
New Skin Co.	Medical	2 1/4"	Cobalt
New Skin Co.	Medical	2 1/4"	Amber
Dr. Kings New Life Pills	Pills	2 1/2"	Clear
Smith Drug Co. Second & James Seattle, Wash.	Medical	2 5/8"	Clear
G. O. Guys PHC Seattle, Wash.	Medical	3 1/4"	Clear
Belt & Son Druggist Salem	Medical	3 1/2"	Clear
	MIDDLE		
Dr. Pierces Tablets For Kidneys & Back Ache	Medical	3 1/2"	Green
The PaPoud Co. New York	Medical	2 3/4"	Cobalt
Plain	Sample Whiskey	4"	Clear
Plain	Sample Whiskey	4 1/2"	Amber
Plain	Sample Whiskey	3 1/2"	Clear
Dr. Shilohs Catarrh Remedy Leroy, N.Y.	Medical	2 1/4"	Aqua
	BOTTOM		
Hall's Catarrh Cure	Medical	4 1/2"	Clear
Hall's Catarrh Medicine	Medical	4 1/2"	Clear
Rubifoam For The Teeth Put Up By E.W. Hoyt & Co. Lowell, Mass.	Tooth Powder	4"	Clear
Watkins Tooth Powder	Tooth Powder	3 1/2"	Clear
Sloan's Liniment	Liniment	5"	Clear
Mexican Mustang Liniment	Liniment	5"	Aqua

EMBOSSING	TOP TYPE	SIZE	COLOR
	TOP		
Plain	Medical	7 1/2"	Blue
Plain	Medical	7 3/8"	Clear
Plain	Acid	6 3/8"	Green
Plain	Medical	7 1/2"	Brown
	BOTTOM		
Plain	Medical Lab Bottle	9 1/4"	Clear
Plain	Medical	9 1/4"	Brown
Plain	Medical	9"	Clear

115

TOP

EMBOSSING	TYPE	SIZE	COLOR
Gilt Edge Dressing	Shoe Polish	3 3/4"	Blue
Climax	Seasoning	3 3/4"	Clear
Thomas Inks L. H. Thomas Co.	Ink	7 1/2"	Green
Sanford's Inks and Library Paste	Ink	9 1/2"	Brown

BOTTOM

Plain	Umbrella Ink	2 1/2"	Aqua
Plain	Boat Ink	1 3/4"	Blue
Plain	Ink	2 3/4"	Blue

EMBOSSING	TYPE	SIZE	COLOR
TOP			
Plain	Ink	2 7/8"	Blue
Plain	Ink	1 7/8"	Amethyst
Plain	Ink	2 3/4"	Amethyst
MIDDLE			
2 OZ.	Ink	2 3/4"	Cobalt
Plain	Ink	2 5/8"	Green
Plain	Ink	2"	Green
BOTTOM			
Plain	Ink	2 1/4"	Amethyst
Plain	Ink	2 1/4"	Amethyst
Plain	Ink	2 1/2"	Amethyst

EMBOSSING	TYPE	SIZE	COLOR
TOP			
Plain	Ink	2 1/2"	Amethyst
Plain	Ink	2 5/8"	Green
S M Co.	Ink	2 5/8"	Amethyst
MIDDLE			
Dovell's Patent	Ink	2 1/2"	Blue
Penn MFG. Works Philada. P. Garrett & Co.	Ink	2"	Milk Glass
J & I E M	Ink	1 3/4"	Blue
BOTTOM			
Plain	Paste	3 1/8"	Aqua
Plain	Paste	3 1/4"	Aqua
Stick Well & Co.	Paste	3"	Aqua

121

EMBOSSING	TYPE	SIZE	COLOR
Ribbed	Pepper Sauce	8 1/2"	Amethyst
Ribbed	Pepper Sauce	8 1/4"	Clear
Ribbed	Pepper Sauce	8 1/4"	Amethyst
Ribbed	Pepper Sauce	8 1/8"	Clear
Ribbed	Pepper Sauce	8"	Amethyst

BOTTOM

Plain	Condiment	9 1/8"	Amber
Plain	Capers	8 3/4"	Green
Charles Gulden New York	Condiment	8 3/4"	Clear
Plain	Capers	8 1/4"	Green
Plain	Pepper Sauce	8"	Blue

TOP

EMBOSSING	TYPE	SIZE	COLOR
Plain	Sauce	7 3/4"	Amethyst
Plain	Cottage Cheese	6 3/4"	Clear
Hirsch's	Pepper Sauce	7 1/4"	Pink
(Label) Ground Cinnamon L.C. Hudson Co. Office, Cor. Front & Pine	Cinnamon	6 3/4"	Blue

BOTTOM

Plain	Olive Oil	7 1/4"	Amethyst
Plain	Castor Oil	6 3/8"	Blue
Plain	Castor Oil	6 1/4"	Blue
Plain	Unknown	8 1/4"	Clear
Plain	Castor Oil	8 1/4"	Amethyst

	TOP		
EMBOSSING	TYPE	SIZE	COLOR
Preferred Stock Catsup Extra Quality	Catsup	10 1/4"	Clear
Columbia Catsup Extra Quality	Catsup	8"	Clear
Plain	Catsup	8 1/8"	Clear
	BOTTOM		
Plain	Catsup	10"	Amethyst
Reifs Special	Catsup	9 1/4"	Brown
Plain	Catsup	9 1/4"	Green

TOP

EMBOSSING	TYPE	SIZE	COLOR
Plain	Olive Oil	11"	Clear
Plain	Olive Oil	9 5/8"	Amethyst
Plain	Olive Oil	9 3/4"	Green
Ermann Olive Oil Ermanns Olive Co. Oroville, Cal.	Olive Oil	9 3/8"	Amethyst

BOTTOM

EMBOSSING	TYPE	SIZE	COLOR
Pure Imported Olive Oil Allen & Lewis Portland, Ore. U.S.A.	Olive Oil	7 3/4"	Green
Pure Imported Olive Oil Allen & Lewis Portland, Ore. U.S.A.	Olive Oil	6 1/4"	Green
Ermann Olive Oil Ermanns Olive Co. Oroville, Cal.	Olive Oil	7 3/4"	Amethyst
Plain	Olive Oil	7 1/4"	Aqua

EMBOSSING	TYPE	SIZE	COLOR
As Shown	Shillings	5 1/8"	Amethyst
As Shown	Shillings	4 1/8"	Amethyst
As Shown	Shillings	3 1/4"	Amethyst
As Shown	Shillings	5 1/8"	Amethyst
As Shown	Shillings	4 1/2"	Amethyst
As Shown	Shillings	3 1/4"	Amethyst

BOTTOM

EMBOSSING	TYPE	SIZE	COLOR
Chesebrough Vaseline Manufact'g Co.	Vaseline	3 1/4"	Clear
Chesebrough MFG. Co. Vaseline	Vaseline	2 5/8"	Amber
Trade Mark Vaseline Chesebrough New York	Vaseline	2 7/8"	Clear
Vaseline Chesebrough New York	Vaseline	2 1/2"	Clear
Vaseline Chesebrough New York	Vaseline	2 7/8"	Brown
Trade Mark Vaseline Chesebrough New York	Vaseline	2 1/2"	Brown

EMBOSSING	TYPE	SIZE	COLOR
	TOP		
Rawleigh's	Extract	8 1/2"	Blue
Rawleigh's Trade Mark	Extract	7 7/8"	Amethyst
Rawleigh's Trade Mark	Extract	6 1/2"	Blue
Rawleigh's	Extract	5 7/8"	Aqua
	BOTTOM		
Ewell's XL Dairy Bottled Milk Co. 21st & Folsom Streets Trade Mark	Milk	6 3/4"	Clear
Plain	Milk	6 1/2"	Clear
Milks' Emulsion	Medical	6 1/4"	Brown
Peptocenic Milk Powder Fairchild Brothers & Foster	Medical	5 7/8"	Brown

TOP

EMBOSSING	TYPE	SIZE	COLOR
Frank Millers Crown Dressing New York U.S.A.	Shoe Polish	5"	Blue
The M.A. Godny Pickling Co. Chicago	Dressing	8"	Clear
My Wife's Salad Dressing, Chicago	Dressing	8"	Clear
E.R. Durkee & Co. Salad Dressing New York	Dressing	6 3/4"	Clear
E.R. Durkee & Co. New York	Dressing	5"	Clear

BOTTOM

EMBOSSING	TYPE	SIZE	COLOR
Plain	Sauce	7 3/8"	Saphire Blue
Trade Mark Chili Powder Gebhardt Eagle	Spice	5 5/8"	Clear
H.J. Heinz Co. Chili Powder Pittsburg U.S.A.	Spice	5 3/8"	Clear
Worcestershire Sauce Lea & Perrins	Sauce	7 1/8"	Green
Worcestershire Sauce Lea & Perrins	Sauce	8 5/8"	Green

TOP

EMBOSSING	TYPE	SIZE	COLOR
Charles Gulden New York	Mustard	3 3/4"	Clear
Charles Gulden Average Capacity 8 OZ. New York	Mustard	3 3/4"	Clear
Charles Gulden New York	Mustard	3 3/4"	Clear

BOTTOM

EMBOSSING	TYPE	SIZE	COLOR
Plain	Mustard	4 1/2"	Amethyst
Chas. Gulden New York	Mustard Seed	3 3/8"	Amethyst
D & Co.	Mustard	4 3/4"	Amethyst

137

TOP

EMBOSSING	TYPE	SIZE	COLOR
Plain Pottery	Unknown	4 1/2"	Brown & Tan
James Keiller & Sons Dundee Marmalade London 1882 Great Britain	Marmalade	4 3/4"	White
Kaukauna Klub It spreads like butter Man'Fd By South Kaukauna Dairy Company Kaukauna, Wisc.	Cheese	4"	Cream
As You Like It Trade Mark Horse-Radish	Horseradish	4"	Brown & Cream

BOTTOM

EMBOSSING	TYPE	SIZE	COLOR
Moutarde Diaphane Louit Freres & Co.	Mustard	5"	Amethyst
Plain	Barrel Mustard	4 1/2"	Amethyst
Plain	Barrel Mustard	4 1/2"	Amethyst

EMBOSSING	TYPE	SIZE	COLOR
16 oz Full Measure J.A. Folger & Co's Golden Gate High Grade Flavoring Extracts	Extract	8"	Clear
2 oz. Full Measure, J.A. Folgers & Co's Golden Gate High Grade Flavoring Extracts	Extract	5 1/2"	Clear
Folger's Golden Gate Flavoring	Extract	6 3/8"	Clear
Folger's Golden Gate Flavoring	Extract	5 1/4"	Clear
J.A. Folger & Co. San Francisco Kansas City	Extract	5 1/8"	Clear

BOTTOM

The Northrop & Sturgis Companys Flavoring Extract	Extract	6 1/4"	Clear
The Northrop & Sturgis Companys Flavoring Extracts Portland, Oregon	Extract	5 3/8"	Clear
Burnett's Standard Flavoring Extracts	Extract	4 1/2"	Clear
Manufactured By the Charles Hires Co.	Root Beer	4 5/8"	Aqua
Hires Root Beer Extract Phidelphia U.S.A.	Root Beer	4 5/8"	Aqua

TOP

EMBOSSING	TYPE	SIZE	COLOR
Dr. Price's Delicious Flavoring Extracts	Extract	5 5/8"	Clear
Burnett's Standard Flavoring Extracts	Extract	5 5/8"	Amethyst
J & F Co.	Extract	6"	Clear
Stearns' Actual Vanilla	Extract	4 5/8"	Clear
M & R Brand Flavors Acme Flavoring Co. Brand Reg. U.S. Pat. Office	Extract	3 7/8"	Clear

BOTTOM

EMBOSSING	TYPE	SIZE	COLOR
Trial Mark Watkins	Extract	8 1/2"	Blue
Watkins	Extract	6 1/4"	Blue
Watkins	Extract	6 1/4"	Clear
Dr. Koch's Dr. Koch Veg. Tea Co. Winona, Minn.	Unknown	7"	Clear

EMBOSSING	TOP		
	TYPE	SIZE	COLOR
Plain	Pickle or Preserves	7 3/4"	Amethyst
Plain	Pickle or Preserves	9 3/4"	Amethyst
Plain	Pickle or Preserves	7 5/8"	Amethyst
	BOTTOM		
Plain	Candy	11 1/2"	Amethyst
Plain	Relish	9"	Amethyst
Plain	Relish	7 3/4"	Amethyst

145

	TOP		
EMBOSSING	TYPE	SIZE	COLOR
Plain	Olive	8"	Amethyst
Plain	Olive	7 1/2"	Amethyst
Plain	Olive	6 3/4"	Amethyst
Plain	Olive	6"	Amethyst
	BOTTOM		
Plain	Olive	9"	Clear
Plain	Olive	8"	Clear
Plain	Olive	6 1/4"	Clear
Plain	Olive	5 1/4"	Amethyst

	TOP		
EMBOSSING	TYPE	SIZE	COLOR
Plain	Pickle	6 1/2"	Green
Plain	Pickle	6 1/4"	Green
Plain	Pickle	6"	Amethyst
Plain	Horse Radish	5 1/2"	Green
	BOTTOM		
Plain	Pickle	8 1/2"	Amethyst
Plain	Pickle	8 1/2"	Aqua
Plain	Pickle	7 1/8"	Clear
Plain	Pickle	7"	Amethyst

EMBOSSING	TYPE	SIZE	COLOR
Horlicks Malted Milk Racine Wis. U.S.A. Slough Bucks, England	Malted Milk	13 1/2"	Green
Horlicks Malted Milk Racine Wis. U.S.A. London, Eng.	Malted Milk	10 3/4"	Green

BOTTOM

Horlicks Malted Milk	Malted Milk	7"	Green
Horlicks Malted Milk	Malted Milk	5"	Green
Horlicks Malted Milk Lunch Tablets	Malted Milk	5"	Clear
Horlicks Malted Milk Lunch Tablets	Malted Milk	5"	Clear
Horlicks Malted Milk Lunch Tablets	Malted Milk	3 1/2"	Clear

TOP

EMBOSSING	TYPE	SIZE	COLOR
Candy Bros. MFG Co. St Louis 4 lbs. Net	Candy	103/4"	Clear
Horlicks Malted Milk Trade M.M.Mark Racine Wis. U.S.A.	Malted Milk	13 1/2"	Clear

BOTTOM

California Casket Company San Francisco, Cal.	Medical	14"	Clear
Plain	Unknown	12 3/4"	Brown

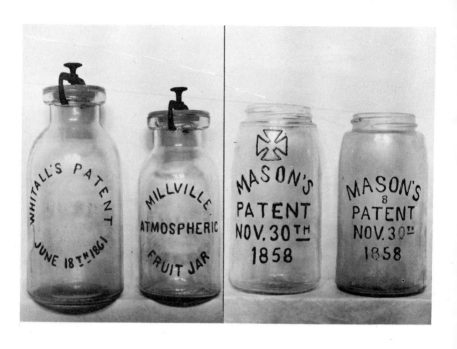

TOP

EMBOSSING	TYPE	SIZE	COLOR
Whitalls Patent Fruit Jar June 18 th 1861 (Back side)	Fruit	9"	Green
Millville Atmospheric Fruit Jar (Front side)	Fruit	8"	Green
Mason's Patent Nov. 30th 1858	Fruit	7"	Green
Mason's 8 Patent Nov. 30th 1858	Fruit	7"	Green

BOTTOM

Mason's Patent Nov. 30th 1858	Fruit	7"	Brown
Safety	Fruit	7"	Brown
Mason's Patent Nov. 30th 1858	Fruit	7"	Green
Mason's Patent Nov. 30th 1858	Fruit	7"	Green

TOP

EMBOSSING	TYPE	SIZE	COLOR
Mason's N Patent Nov. 30th 1858	Fruit	7"	Green
Mason's Patent Nov. 30th 1858	Fruit	7"	Green
Mason's Patent Nov. 30th 1858	Fruit	9"	Green
Atlas Mason's Patent Nov. 30th 1858	Fruit	9"	Green

BOTTOM

The Marion Jar Mason's Patent Nov. 30th 1858	Fruit	7"	Green
Ball Mason's Patent 1858	Fruit	7"	Green
Atlas Mason's Patent	Fruit	7"	Green
Mason	Fruit	7"	Green

TOP

EMBOSSING	TYPE	SIZE	COLOR
Economy Trade Mark	Fruit	6 5/8"	Amethyst
Improved Everlasting Jar	Fruit	6 1/2"	Amethyst
The Gem	Fruit	8 1/2"	Green
Woodbury	Fruit	9"	Green

BOTTOM

Standard Mason	Fruit	7"	Green
Root Mason	Fruit	7"	Green
Trade Mark Lightning	Fruit	9 3/4"	Green
Globe	Fruit	7 1/2"	Brown

EMBOSSING	TYPE	SIZE	COLOR
		TOP	
Masons Improved	Fruit	5 1/2"	Green
Gem	Fruit	5 1/2"	Green
Mason's Patent Nov. 30th 1858	Fruit	5 1/2"	Green
Mason's Patent Nov. 30th 1858	Fruit	5 1/2"	Green
		BOTTOM	
Sun Trade Mark	Fruit	7"	Aqua
Sun Trade Mark	Fruit	5 3/4"	Aqua
San Francisco Glass Works	Fruit	8 1/2"	Aqua
Mason's Patent Nov. 30th 1858	Fruit	9"	Aqua

This bottle was dug up at Angels Camp, California

FIGURAL BOTTLES

COMMEMORATIVE BOTTLES

UNUSUAL BOTTLES

Left to Right

1. Emerald Green Bottle; 2. Black Russian Bear;
3. Spanish Drinking Bottle.

UNUSUAL BOTTLES

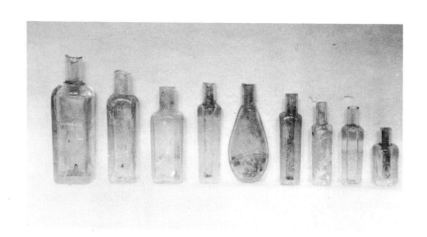

CHINESE ITEMS

Top to Bottom

1. Opium Bottles; 2. Opium Pipe; 3. Chinese Ware

Left to Right   COLLECTABLE ITEMS

1. Curling Iron; 2. Coal Oil Lamp; 3. Gas Lamp Shade;
4. Gas Lamp Shade.

COLLECTABLE ITEMS

Top: Glass Insulators – Bottom: Caboose Lantern

COLLECTABLE ITEMS

Top: Toys — Bottom: Carbide Cans, Fire Hose Nozzle

COLLECTABLE ITEMS

Top: Cork Puller — Bottom: Cork Taperer

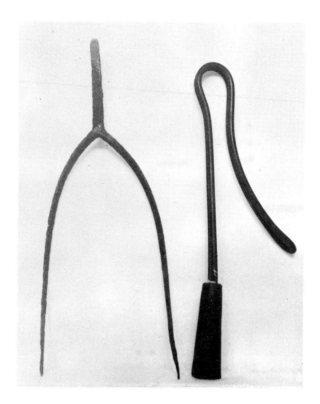

COLLECTABLE ITEMS
Top: Pitch Fork, Sheep Crook – Bottom: Gun Barrels

COLLECTABLE ITEMS

Top: Indian Artifacts – Bottom: Assay Crucibles

COLLECTABLE ITEMS

Top: 60 lb. Cannon Ball – Bottom: Copper Ingot

Author and Burro heading out for more bottles and pictures.

The following are a list of old Beverages and Remedy recipes, that were popular and widely used during the early 1800's, until middle 1900. If you wish to try any of the following recipes, we ask that you do so at your own risk, for we will not be held responsible.

BEVERAGES [1]

Florida Orange Wine:
Wipe the oranges with a wet cloth, peel off the yellow rind very thin, squeeze the oranges, and strain the juice through a hair-sieve; measure the juice after it is strained and for each gallon allow three pounds of granulated sugar, the white and shell of one egg and one-third of a gallon of cold water; put the sugar, the white and shell of the egg (crushed small) and the water over the fire and stir them every two minutes until the eggs begin to harden; then boil the syrup until it looks clear under the froth of egg which will form on the surface; strain the syrup, pour it upon the orange rind and let it stand over night; then next add the orange juice and again let it stand over night; strain it the second day, and put it into a tight cask with a small cake of compressed yeast to about ten gallons of wine, and leave the bung out of the cask until the wine ceases to ferment; the hissing noise continues as long as fermentation is in progress; when fermentation ceases, close the cask by driving in the bung, and let the wine stand about nine months before bottling it; three months after it is bottled, it can be used. A glass of brandy added to each gallon of wine after fermentation ceases is generally considered an improvement.

Black Currant Wine
Four quarts of whisky, four quarts of black currants, four pounds of brown or white sugar, one tablespoonful of cloves, one tablespoonful of cinnamon.
Crush the currants and let them stand in the whisky with the spices for three weeks; then strain and add the sugar; set away again for three weeks longer; then strain and bottle.

Cherry Bounce
To one gallon of wild cherries add enough good whisky to cover the fruit. Let soak two or three weeks and then drain off the liquor. Mash the cherries without breaking the stones and strain through a jelly-bag; add this liquor to that already drained off. Make a syrup with a gill of water and a pound of white sugar to every two quarts of liquor thus prepared; stir in well and bottle, and tightly cork. A common way of making cherry bounce is to put wild cherries and whisky together in a jug and use the liquor as wanted.

Blackberry Cordial
Warm and squeeze the berries; add to one pint of juice one pound of white sugar, one-half ounce of powdered cinnamon, one-fourth ounce of mace, two teaspoonfuls of cloves. Boil all together for one-fourth of an hour; strain the syrup, and to each pint add a glass of French brandy. Two or three doses of a tablespoonful or less will check any slight diarrhoea. When the attack is violent, give a tablespoonful after each discharge until the complaint is in subjection. It will ar-

rest dysentery if given in season, and is a pleasant and safe remedy. Excellent for children when teething.

Hop Beer

Take five quarts of water, six ounces of hops, boil it three hours; then strain the liquor, add to it five quarts of water, four ounces of bruised ginger root; boil this again twenty minutes, strain and add four pounds of sugar. When luke-warm put in a pint of yeast. Let it ferment; in twenty-four hours it will be ready for bottling.

Ginger Beer

Put into a kettle two ounces of powdered ginger root (or more if it is not very strong), half an ounce of cream of tartar, two large lemons, cut in slices, two pounds of broken loaf sugar and two gallons of soft boiling water. Simmer them over a slow fire for half an hour. When the liquor is nearly cold, stir into it a large tablespoonful of the best yeast. After it has fermented, which will be in about twenty-four hours, bottle for use.

Spruce Beer

Allow an ounce of hops and a spoonful of ginger to a gallon of water. When well boiled, strain it and put in a pint of molasses, or a pound of brown sugar, and half an ounce or less of the essence of spruce; when cool, add a teacupful of yeast and put into a clean tight cask, and let it ferment for a day or two, then bottle it for use. You can boil the sprigs of spruce fir in place of the essence.

Roman Punch

Grate the yellow rind of four lemons and two oranges upon two pounds of loaf sugar. Squeeze the juice of the lemons and oranges; cover it and let it stand until next day. Strain it through a sieve, mix with the sugar; add a bottle of champagne and the whites of eight eggs beaten to a stiff froth. It may be frozen or not, as desired. For winter use snow instead of ice.

Delicious Junket

Take two quarts of new milk, warm it on the stove to about blood heat, pour it into a glass or china bowl and stir into it two tablespoonfuls of prepared rennet, two tablespoonsful of powdered loaf sugar, add a small wine-glassful of pale brandy. Let it stand till cold and eat with sugar and rich cream. Half the quantity can be made.

Strawberry Shrub

One quart of raspberry juice, half a pound of loaf sugar, dissolved, a pint of Jamaica rum, or part rum and brandy. Mix thoroughly. Bottle for use.

Sassafras Mead

Mix gradually with two quarts of boiling water three pounds and a half of the best brown sugar, a pint and a half of good West India molasses, and a quarter of a pound of tataric acid. Stir it well and when cool, strain it into a large jug

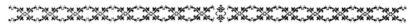

or pan, then mix in a teaspoonful (not more) of essence of sassafras. Transfer it to clean bottles (it will fill about half a dozen), cork it tightly and keep it in a cool place. It will be fit for use next day. Put into a box or boxes a quarter of a pound of carbonate of soda, to use with it. To prepare a glass of sassafras mead for drinking, put a large tablespoonful of the mead into a half tumbler full of ice-water, stir into it a half teaspoonful of the soda and it will immediately foam up to the top.

Sassafras mead will be found a cheap, wholesome and pleasant beverage for warm weather. The essence of sassafras, tartaric acid and carbonate of soda, can, of course, all be obtained at the druggist's.

Cream Soda Without The Fountain
Coffee-sugar, four pounds, three pints of water, three nutmegs, grated, the whites of ten eggs, well-beaten, gum arabic, one ounce, twenty drops of oil of lemon, or extract equal to that amount. By using oils of other fruits, you can make as many flavors from this as you desire. Mix all and place over a gentle fire, and stir well about thirty minutes; remove from the fire and strain, and divide into two parts; into one-half put eight ounces of bi-carbonate of soda, into the other half put six ounces of tartaric acid. Shake well, and when cold they are ready for use by pouring three or four spoonfuls from both parts into seperate glasses, each one-third full of water. Stir each and pour together, and you have a nice glass of cream soda which you can drink at your leisure, as the gum and eggs hold the gas.

For A Summer Draught
The juice of one lemon, a tumblerful of cold water, pounded sugar to taste, half a small teaspoonful of carbonate of soda. Squeeze the juice from the lemon; strain and add it to the water, with sufficient pounded sugar to sweeten the whole nicely. When well mixed, put in the soda, stir well and drink while the mixture is in an effervescing state.

Noyeau Cordial
To one gallon of proof spirit add three pounds of loaf sugar and a tablespoonful of extract of almounds. Mix well together and allow to stand forty-eight hours, covered closely; now strain through thick flannel and bottle. This liquor will be much improved by adding half a pint of apricot or peach juice.

Egg Nogg
Beat the yolks of twelve eggs very light, stir in as much white sugar as they will dissolve, pour in gradually one glass of brandy to cook the eggs, one glass of old whisky, one grated nutmeg, and three pints of rich milk. Beat the whites to a froth and stir in last.

Egg Flip, or Mulled Ale
Boil one quart of good ale with some nutmeg; beat up six eggs and mix them with a little cold ale; then pour the hot ale to it, and pour it back and forth several times to prevent its curdling; warm and stir it till sufficiently thick; add a piece of butter or a glass of brandy and serve it with dry toast.

Milk Punch

One pint of milk made very sweet; a wine-glassful of brandy or rum, well stirred together; grate a little nutmeg over the top of the glasses. Serve with a straw in each glass.

Strawberry Water

Take one cupful of ripe hulled berries; crush with a wooden spoon, mixing with a mass a quarter of a pound of pulverized sugar and half a pint of cold water. Pour the mixture into a fine sieve, rub through and filter till clear; add the strained juice of one lemon and one and one half pints of cold water, mix thoroughly and set in ice chest till wanted.

This makes a nice, cool drink on a warm day and easily to be made in strawberry season.

Koumiss

Koumiss is prepared by dissolving four ounces of white sugar in one gallon of skimmed milk, and placing in bottles of the capacity of one quart; add two ounces of bakers' yeast, or a cake of compressed yeast to each bottle. Cork and tie securely, set in a warm place until fermentation is well under way, and lay the bottles on their sides in a cool cellar. In three days, fermentation will have progressed sufficiently to permit the koumiss to be in good condition.

Very Strong Table Vinegar

Take two gallons of good cider and thoroughly mix it with two pounds of new honey, pour into your cask or bottle and let it stand from four to six months, when you will have vinegar so strong that it cannot be used at table without diluting with water. It is the best ever procured for pickling purpose.

Inexpensive Drink

A very nice, cheap drink which may take the place of lemonade and be found fully as healthful is made with one cupful of pure cider vinegar, half a cupful of good molasses, put into one quart pitcher of ice-water. A tablespoonful of ground ginger added makes a healthful beverage.

TOILET RECIPES, ITEMS [1]

Cologne Water

Oil of lavender two drachms, oil of rosemary one drachm and a half, ornage, lemon and bergamot, one drachm each of the oil; also two drachms of the essence of musk, attar of rose ten drops, and a pint of proof spirit. Shake all together thoroughly three times a day for a week.

Jockey Club Bouquet

Mix one pint extract of rose, one pint extract of tuberose, half a pint of extract of cassia, four ounces extract of jasmine, and three ounces tincture of civet. Filter the mixture.

Rose Water
Preferable to the distilled for a perfume, or for culinary purposes. Alter of rose, twelve drops; rub it up with half an ounce of white sugar and two drachms carbonate magnesia; then add gradually one quart of water and two ounces of proof spirit, and filter through paper.

Bay Rum
French proof spirit one gallon, extract bay six ounces. Mix and color with caramel; needs no filtering.

Lavender Water
Oil of lavender two ounces, orris root half an ounce, spirits of wine one pint. Mix and keep two or three weeks. It may then be strained through two thicknesses of blotting paper and is ready for use.

Cream Of Lillies
Best white castor oil; pour in a little strong solution of sal tartar in water, and shake it until it looks thick and white. Perfume with lavender.

Cream Of Roses
Olive oil one pound, attar of roses fifty drops, oil of rosemary twenty-five drops; mix, and color it with alkanet root.

Cold Cream
Melt one ounce oil of almonds, half ounce spermaceti, one drachm white wax, and then add two ounces of rose-water, and stir it constantly until cold.

Hair Invigorator
Bay rum two pints, alcohol one pint, castor oil one ounce, carb. ammonia half an ounce, tincture of cantharides one ounce. Mix them well. This compound will promote the growth of the hair and prevent it from falling out.

Dye For White Or Light Eyebrows
Boil an ounce of walnut bark in a pint of water for an hour. Add a lump of alum the size of a filbert, and when cold, apply with a camel's-hair brush.

Hair Wash
One penny's worth of borax, half a pint of olive oil, one pint of boiling water.

Pour the boiling water over the borax and oil; let it cool; then put the mixture into a bottle. Shake it before using, and apply it with a flannel. Camphor and borax, dissolved in boiling water and left to cool, make a very good wash for the hair; as also does rosemary water mixed with a little borax. After using any of these washes, when the hair becomes thoroughly dry, a little pomatum or oil should be rubbed in to make it smooth and glossy-that is, if one prefers oil on the hair.

Ox-Marrow Pomade For The Hair

One marrow bone, half a pint of oil, ten cents' worth of citronella. Take the marrow out of the bone, place it in warm water, let it get almost to boiling point, then let it cool and pour the water away; repeat this three times until the marrow is thoroughly "fined". Beat the marrow to a cream with a silver fork, stir the oil in, drop by drop, beating all the time; when quite cold add the citronella, pour into jars and cover down.

To Increase The Hair in the Brows

Clip them and annoint with a little sweet oil. Should the hair fall out, having been full, use one of the hair invigorators.

Pearl Tooth Powder

Prepared chalk half a pound, powdered myrrh two ounces, camphor two drachms, orris root, powdered, two ounces; moisten the camphor with alcohol and mix well together.

Bad Breath

Bad breath from catarrh, foul stomach, or bad teeth, may be temporarily relieved by diluting a little bromo chloralum with eight or ten parts of water, and using it as a gargle, and swallowing a few drops before going out. A pint of bromo chloralum costs fifty cents, but a small vial will last a long time.

Shaving Compound

Half a pound a plain, white soap, dissolved in a small quantity of alcohol, as little as can be used; add a tablespoonful of pulverized borax. Shave the soap and put it in a small tin basin or cup; place it on the fire in a dish of boiling water; when melted, add the alchohol, and remove from the fire; stir in oil of bergamot sufficient to perfume it.

Barber's Shampoo Mixture

Dissolve half an ounce of carbonate of ammonia and one ounce of borax in one quart of water; then add two ounces of glycerine in three quarts of New England rum, and one quart of bay rum. Moisten the hair with this liquid, shampoo with the hands until a light lather is formed; then wash off with plenty of clean water.

Odoriferous or Sweet-Scenting Bags

Lavender flowers one ounce, pulverized orris two dachms, bruised rosemary leaves half ounce, musk five grains, attar of rose five drops. Mix well, sew up in small flat muslin bags, and cover them with fancy silk or satin.

These are very nice to keep in your bureau drawers or trunk, as the perfume penetrates through the contents of the trunk or drawers. An acceptable present to a single gentleman.

Toilet Soap

One pound of washing soda, one pound of lard or clear tallow, half a pound of unslacked lime, one tablespoonful of salt, three quarts of water. Put the soda

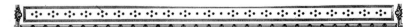

and lime in a large dish, and pour over the water, boiling hot; stir until dissolved; let it stand until clear, then pour off the clear liquid, add the grease and salt; boil four hours, then pour into pans to cool. If it should be inclined to curdle or separate, indicating the lime to be too strong, pour in a little more water, and boil again. Perfume as you please, and pour into molds or a shallow dish, and, when cold, cut into bars to dry.

REMEDYS [1]

Draughts For The Feet
Take a large leaf from the horse-radish plant, and cut out the hard fibres that run through the leaf; place it on a hot shovel for a moment to soften it, fold it, and fasten it closely in the hollow of the foot by a cloth bandage.

Burdock leaves, cabbage leaves, and mullein leaves, are used in the same manner, to alleviate pain and promote perspiration.

Garlics are also made for draughts by pounding them, placing them on a hot tin plate for a moment to sweat them, and binding them closely to the hollow of the foot by a cloth bandage.

Draughts of onions, for infants, are made by roasting onions in hot ashes, and, when they are quite soft, peeling off the outside, mashing them, and applying them on a cloth as usual.

A Remedy For Boils
An excellent remedy for boils is water of a temperature agreeable to the feelings of the patient. Apply wet linen to the part affected and frequently renew or moisten it. It is said to be the most effectual remedy known. Take inwardly some good blood purifier.

Cure For Ringworms
Yellow dock, root or leaves, steeped in vinegar, will cure the worst case of ringworms.

HEALTH SUGGESTIONS [1]

Growing Pains Cured
Following in our mother's footsteps, we have been routed night after night from our warm quarters, in the dead of winter, to kindle fires and fill frosty kettles, from water-pails thickly crusted with ice, that we might get the writhing pedal extremities of our little heir into a tub of water as quickly as possible. But lately we have learned that all this work and exposure is needless. We simply wring a towel from salted water- a bowl of it standing in our sleeping room, ready for such an emergency-wrap the limb in it from the ankle to knee, without taking the child from his bed, and then swathe with dry flannels, thick and warm, tucking the blankets about him a little closer, and relief is sure.

How To Keep Well

Don't sleep in a draught.
Don't go to bed with cold feet.
Don't eat what you do not need, just to save it.
Don't stand over hot-air registers.
Don't stuff a cold lest you should be next obliged to starve a fever.
Don't sit in a damp or chilly room without a fire.
Don't try to get along without flannel underclothing in winter.

Colds and Hoarseness

Borax has proved a most effective remedy in certain forms of colds. In sudden hoarseness or loss of voice in public speakers or singers, from colds, relief for an hour or so may be obtained by slowly dissolving, and partially swallowing, a lump of borax the size of a garden pea, or about three or four grains held in the mouth for ten or fifteen minutes before speaking or singing. This produces a profuse secretion of saliva or "watering" of the mouth and throat, just as wetting brings back the missing notes to a flute when it is too dry.

A flannel dipped in boiling water and sprinkled with turpentine, laid on chest as wuickly as possible, will relieve the most severe cold or hoarseness.

Another simple, pleasant remedy is furnished by beating up the white of one egg, adding to it the juice of one lemon, and sweetening with white sugar to taste. Take a teaspoonful from time to time. It has been known to effectually cure the ailment.

Or bake a lemon or sour orange twenty minutes in a moderate oven. When done, open at one end and take out the inside. Sweeten with sugar or molasses. This is an excellent remedy for hoarseness.

An old time and good way to relieve a cold is to go to bed and stay there, drinking nothing, not even water, for twenty-four hours, and eating as little as possible. Or go to bed, put your feet in hot mustard and water, put a bran or oatmeal poultice on the chest, take ten grains of Dover's powder, and an hour afterwards a pint of hot gruel; in the morning, rub the body all over with a coarse towel, and take a dose of aperient medicine.

Molasses Posset

This old-fashioned remedy for a cold is an effectual now as it was in old times. Put into a saucepan a pint of the best West India molasses, a teaspoonful of powdered white ginger and a quarter of a pound of fresh butter. Set it over the fire and simmer it slowly for half an hour, stirring it frequently. Do not let it come to a boil. Then stir in the juice of two lemons, or two tablespoonfuls of vinegar; cover the pan and let it stand by the fire five minutes longer. This is good for a cold. Some of it may be taken warm at once, and the remainder kept at hand for occasional use. It is the preparation absurdly called by the common people a stewed quaker.

Cough Syrup

Syrup of squills four ounces, syrup of tolu four ounces, tincture of bloodroot one and one-half ounces, camphorated tincture of opium four ounces. Mix. Dose

for an adult, one teaspoonful repeated every two to four hours, or as often as necessary.

Leanness
Is caused generally by lack of power in the digestive organs to digest and assimilate the fat-producing elements of food. First restore digestion, take plenty of sleep, drink all the water stomach will bear in the morning on rising, take moderate exercise in the open air, eat oatmeal, cracked wheat, graham mush, baked sweet apples, roasted and broiled beef. Cultivate jolly people, and bathe daily.

For Toothache
The worst toothache, or neuralgia, coming from the teeth may be speedily and delightfully ended by the application of a bit of clean cotton saturated in a solution of ammonia to the defective tooth. Sometimes the late sufferer is prompted to momentary laughter by the application, but the pain will disappear.

To Cure Earache
Take a bit of cotton batting, put on it a pinch of black pepper, gather it up and tie it, dip it in sweet oil, and insert it in the ear; put a flannel bandage over the head to keep it warm; it often gives immediate relief.

Tobacco smoke, puffed into the ear, has oftentimes been effectual.

Another remedy: Take equal parts of tincture of opium and glycerine. Mix, and from a warm teaspoon drop two or three drops into the ear, stop the ear tight with cotton, and repeat every hour or two. If matter should form in the ear, make a suds with castile soap and warm water, about 100 degrees F., or a little more than milk warm, and have some person inject it into the ear while you hold that side of the head the lowest. If it does not heal in due time, inject a little carbolic acid and water in the proportion of one drachm of the acid to one pint of warm water each time after using the suds.

Relief From Asthma
Sufferers from asthma should get a muskrat skin and wear it over their lungs with the fur side next to the body. It will bring certain relief. Or soak blotting paper in saltpetre water, then dry, burning at night in the patient's bedroom.

Another excellent recipe: Take powdered liquorice root, powdered elecampane root, powdered anise-seed, each one drachm, powdered ipecac ten grains, powdered lobelia ten grains; add sufficient amount of tar to form into pills of ordinary size. Take three or four pills on going to bed. An excellent remedy for asthma or shortness of breath.

Recipes For Felons
Take common rock salt, as used for salting down pork or beef, dry in an oven, then pound it fine and mix with spirits of turpentine in equal parts; put it in a rag and wrap it around the parts affected; as it gets dry put on more, and in twenty-four hours you are cured. The felon will be dead.

Or purchase the herb of stramonium at the druggist's steep it and bind it on

the felon; as soon as cold, put on new, warm herbs. It will soon kill it in a few hours at least.

Or saturate a bit of grated wild turnip, the size of a bean, with spirits of turpentine, and apply it to the affected part. It relieves the pain at once; in twelve hours there will be a hole to the bone, and the felon destroyed; then apply healing salve, and the finger is well.

A simple remedy for felons, relieving pain at once, no poulticing, no cutting, no "holes to the bone", no necessity for healing salve, but simple oil of cedar applied a few times at the commencement of the felon, and the work is done.

To take Cinders from the Eye

In most cases a simple and effective cure may be found in one or two grains of flax-seed, which can be placed in the eye without pain or injury. As they dissolve, a glutinous substance is formed; which envelops any foreign body that may be under the lid, and the whole is easily washed out. A dozen of these seeds should constitute a part of every traveler's outfit.

Another remedy for removing objects from the eye: Take a horsehair and double it leaving a loop. If the object can be seen, lay the loop over it, close the eye, and the mote will come out as the hair is withdrawn. This method is practiced by axemakers and other workers in steel.

Sunstroke

Wrap a wet cloth bandage over the head; wet another cloth, folded small, square, cover it thickly with salt, and bind it on the back of the neck; apply dry salt behind the ears. Put mustard plasters to the calves of the legs and soles of the feet. This is an effectual remedy.

Swaim's Vermifuge

Woem seed, two ounces; valerian, rhubarb, pink root, white agaric, senna, of each one ounce and a half. Boil in sufficient water to yield three quarts of decoction. Now add to it ten drops of the oil of tansy and forty-five drops of the oil of cloves, dissolved in a quart of rectified spirit. Dose: one tablespoonful at night.

Camphorated Oil

Best oil of Lucca, gum camphor. Pound some gum camphor and fill a wide-necked pint bottle one-third full; fill up with olive oil and set away until the camphor is absorbed. Excellent lotion for sore chest, sore throat, aching limbs, etc.

"The Suns" Cholera Mixture

More than forty years ago, when it was found that prevention for the Asiatic cholera was easier than cure, the learned doctors of both hemispheres drew up a prescription, which was published *for working people) in The New York Sun, and took the name of "The Sun Cholera Mixture". It is found to be the best remedy for looseness of the bowels ever yet devised. It is to be commended for several reasons. It is not to be mixed with liquor, and therefore will not be used as an alcoholic beverage. Its ingredients are well known among all common people, and it will have no prejudice to combat; each of the materials is in equal proportions to the

others, and it may therefore be compounded without professional skill; and as the
dose is so very small, it may be carried in a tiny phial in the waistcoat pocket, and
be always at hand. It is:

Take equal parts of tincture of cayenne, tincture of opium, tincture of rhubarb, essence of peppermint and spirits of camphor. Mix well. Dose fifteen to
thirty drops in a wine-glass of water, according to age and violence of the attack.
Repeat every fifteen or twenty minutes until relief is obtained. No one who takes
it in time will ever have the cholera. Even when no cholera is anticipated, it is a
valuable remedy for ordinary summer complaints, and should always be kept in
readiness.

Comp. Cathartic Elixir

The only pleasant and reliable cathartic in liquid form than can be prescrib-
ed.

Each fluid ounce contains: Sulph. magnesia one drachm, senna two drachms,
scammony six grains, liquorice one drachm, ginger three grains, coriander five
grains, with flavoring ingredients. Dose. -Child five years old, one or two teaspoonfuls; adult, one or two tablespoonfuls.

This preparation is being used extensively throughout the country. It was or-
iginated with the design of furnishing a liquid cathartic remedy that could be pre-
scribed in a palatable form. It will be taken by children with a relish.

Grandmother's Cough Syrup

Take half a pound of dry hoarhound herbs, one pod of red pepper, four tablespoonful of good, fresh tar and a pound of sugar. Boil slowly and stir often, until
it is reduced to one quart of syrup. When cool, bottle for use. Take one or two
teaspoonfuls four or six times a day.

Grandmother's Universal Liniment

One pint of alcohol and as much camphor gum as can be dissolved in it, half
an ounce of the oil of cedar, one-half ounce of the oil of sassafras, aqua ammonia
half an ounce, and the same amount of the tincture of morphine. Shake well together and apply by the fire; the liniment must not be heated, or come in contact
with the fire, but the rubbing to be done by the warmth of the fire.

These recipes of Grandmother's are all old, tried medicines, and are more
effectual than most of those that are advertised, as they have been thoroughly tried
and proved reliable.

Grandmother's Family Spring Bitters

Mandrake root one ounce, dandelion root one ounce, burdock root one ounce,
yellow dock root one ounce, prickly ash berries two ounces, marsh mallow one
ounce, turkey rhubarb half an ounce, gentian one ounce, English camomile flowers
one ounce, red clover tops two ounces.

Wash the herbs and roots; put them into earthen vessel, pour over two quarts
of water that has been boiled and cooled; let it stand over night and soak; in the
morning, set it on the back of the stove, and steep it five hours; it must not boil,
but be nearly ready to boil. Strain it through a cloth, and add half a pint of good

gin. Keep it in a cool place. Half a wine-glass taken as a dose twice a day.

This is better than all the patent blood medicines that are in the market - a superior blood purifier, and will cure almost any malignant sore, by taking according to direction, and washing the sore with a strong tea of red raspberry leaves steeped, first washing the sore with castile soap, then drying with a soft cloth, and washing it with the strong tea of red raspberry leaves.

Grandmother's Eye-Wash

Take three fresh eggs and break them into one quart of clear, cold rain-water; stir until thoroughly mixed; bring to a boil on a slow fire, stirring often; then add half an ounce of sulphate of zinc (white vitriol) continue the boiling for two minutes, then set it off the fire. Take the curd that settles at the bottom of this and apply to the eye at night with a bandage. It will speedily draw out all fever and soreness. Strain the liquid through a cloth and use for bathing the eyes occasionally. This is the best eye-water ever made for man or beast. I have used it for twenty years without knowing it to fail.

HINTS IN REGARD TO HEALTH [1]

It is plainly seen by an inquiring mind that, aside from the selection and preparation of food, there are many little things constantly arising in the experience of everyday life which, in their combined effect, are powerful agents in the formation (or prevention) of perfect health. A careful observance of these little occurrences, an inquiry into the philosophy attending them, lies within the province, and indeed should be considered among the highest duties, of every housekeeper.

That the flavor of cod-liver oil may be changed to the delightful one of fresh oyster, if the patient will drink a large glass of water poured from a vessel in which nails have been allowed to rust.

That warm borax water will remove dandruff.

That a bag of hot sand relieves neuralgia.

That salt should be eaten with nuts to aid digestion.

That a cupful of strong coffee will remove the odor of onions from the breath.

A cupful of hot water drank before meals will relieve nausea and dyspepsia.

That one in a faint should be laid flat on his back, then loosen his clothes and let him alone.

For a cold in the head, nothing is better than powdered borax, sniffed up the nostrils.

Whooping cough paroxysms are relieved by breathing the fumes of turpentine and carbolic acid.

For stomach cramps, ginger ale or a teaspoonful of tincture of ginger in a half glass of water in which a half teaspoonful of soda has been dissolved.

Sickness of the stomach is most promptly relieved by drinking a teacupful of hot soda and water. If it brings the offending matter up, all the better.

TABLE MANNERS FOR CHILDREN

If you dine with your master, let him begin first; don't press up too high, but take the place assigned to you. At the table don't pare your nails. If your master speaks to you, take off your cap and stand up. Try your soup before putting bread in it; if another shares your dish, don't crumble bread in it, as your hands may be sweaty. Cut nice bits of bread to put in your broth, and don't sup that too loudly. Don't dip your meat in the common salt-cellar, wipe your spoon clean before putting it down, and take care that it be not stolen. Burnish no bones with your teeth. Belch near to no man's face; don't scratch your head at meals; don't spit over the table; or pick your teeth with a knife. Wipe your mouth when you drink. Don't blow your nose on your napkin. Don't fill your mouth too full, or blow out your crumbs. Don't blow on you soup or drink, "for if thou be not whole of thy body, thy breath is corruptible." "Cast not thy bones under the Table." Don't stretch at the table, nor cut the table with your knife. When leaving the table say to your companions, "Much good do it ye," bow to your master and withdraw.[2]

---

[1] Hugo Ziemann and Mrs. F. L. Gillette, The White House Cook Book, (1887).

[2] Frederick J. Furnivall (editor), The Babees Book (1886).

Adolphson's
PRINTING CO.

SALEM, OREGON